MEMORIES OF A STAY IN THE COUNTRY

Peggy Edna Nash

MINERVA PRESS

LONDON

MONTREUX   LOS ANGELES   SYDNEY

MEMORIES OF A STAY IN THE COUNTRY
Copyright © Peggy Edna Nash 1997

ISBN 1 86106 900 6

First Published 1997 by
MINERVA PRESS
315–317 Regent Street
London W1R 7YB

Printed in Great Britain for Minerva Press

With best wishes,

Peggy Edna Nash

MEMORIES OF A STAY IN
THE COUNTRY

Thoughts come of all the yesterdays –
Memories of them stream.
But what of all the yesterdays –
Are they what they seem?
O where are all the yesterdays –
Or were they just a dream?

Dedicated with love to my dear grandchildren

Contents

Chapter One

Evacuation

Towards the end of August 1939, as a fourteen year old returning home from secretarial college, I saw a placard outside a local newsagent's. It read, WAR IS IMMINENT.

The next day, usually early closing, the shops were kept open so that our parents could buy one day's supply of food ready for our evacuation to the country.

On Friday the first of September 1939, my colleagues and I, each carrying our gas mask, together with a suitcase containing items of warm clothing, boarded a train from outer London. The destination was unknown. Having been supplied with barley sugar for travel sickness and sufficient food for a whole day, we were fully expecting a long journey. To our surprise, less than fifteen miles away we alighted at Sevenoaks in Kent. "I cycle down here!" came a rather disgruntled voice, expecting the excitement of more 'foreign' regions – the Welsh mountains, perhaps? However, Sevenoaks it was, which, as my stay was to last over two years, at least had the advantage of being near enough to allow me to spend the holidays at home.

On leaving the station, we were taken in various cars to a local hall. When we were split into groups, I found myself unable to join the one for which I had hoped. Thinking myself to be the only one not fitted into a billet, I looked around and found another, quite new, student on her own. A kind lady bundled both of us off and drove us to a large house in a wooded avenue.

Obviously not expected, we were not made to feel very comfortable. We were told that food would get very short. On finding that my friend Joan, aged thirteen, had brought a mountain of sandwiches with her, we had to live on these for what seemed like days.

On Sunday the third of September 1939, we were taken to the nearby Seal Church. Hats being a 'must' in those days, I was given a large-brimmed straw hat to wear – how conspicuous I felt! Halfway through the service a loud wailing noise could be heard outside, the first of many air raid warnings we were to hear over the next few years. The church service was brought to an early, though discreet, end. Outside, and for the first time, I saw a tin hat, which was being worn by an anxious-looking policeman on point duty.

When we arrived back, the gentleman of the house was nowhere to be seen. Our agitated hostess searched the large garden to no avail. She spoke to us of German weapons which travelled silently and caused one to disappear into the ground, never to be seen again! (Could she have been foretelling the V2 rocket we were to be bombarded with years later?) Just then, the lady's husband appeared from the outskirts of the grounds completely unruffled and, thankfully, there was no sign of a secret weapon having landed!

The air raid warning proved to be a false alarm, but was rather mystifying to us, as it was only when we listened to the wireless later that we heard the news. At 11 o'clock that morning (just as our church service was starting, and so unknown to us), the Prime Minister, Mr Neville Chamberlain, had broadcast to the Nation that we were at war with Germany.

The next day, Monday, our hostess told us we had better go out and look for some of our college friends, as we should be starting our studies again. The Billeting Committee had given her no information on where we could find our tutor, nor did they let him know where we had been sent. Joan and I set off down the avenue and, as luck would have it, decided to turn right at the end. About half a mile on, suddenly and to our great relief, we saw two of our friends blackberrying by the roadside. Betty and Effie told us that our tutor was very worried about what had happened to us and that if anyone saw us we were to be sent to him immediately. We reached his house with some trepidation, which was justified as he was quite cross with us. However, we eventually managed to convince him that it was not our fault we had been 'lost', so all was well after all.

Our stay in the avenue was not very pleasant, both of us being expected to carry out many domestic tasks – cleaning, mainly. We felt in a state of limbo, and very far from home. After two weeks we were told that our hostess' brother was very ill in Ireland, and she and her husband had to leave straight away.

We were then sent to a very nice couple who did their best to make us happy. The popular tune at the time was *Run Rabbit, Run*, which was soon given the words 'Run Adolf, Run'. It was, of course, found amusing to make fun of Germany's dictator, Adolf Hitler.

There was some concern one evening when, suddenly, I let out a yell. A dozy wasp had crawled out from between the settee seat cushions and stung the back of my calf! The poison was nobly sucked out and no harm was done.

One afternoon two weeks later, whilst we were having tea, the billeting officer called. She asked if we would mind moving to a place nearby, where two of our girls were billeted with two students from Dulwich College. She asked us to exchange with them to keep the colleges together. We were very happy where we were, but of course thought we had to say that we would not mind. When the lady had gone, our hostess told us that if she had known beforehand, she would have told us to say no.

We were then sent to our third and final billet. It was a small three-bedroomed house occupied by Mr and Mrs 'M' and their two daughters, who shared the same names as ourselves, Joan and Peggy. Also billeted there were Betty and Effie, whom we had found picking blackberries a few weeks before.

Peggy was eighteen years old. Joan had had her twelfth birthday on the day the war started (third of September 1939). It was also the birth-date of my friend Joan's father. (Fifty-four years later I was to have a grandson, Shaun, born on the third of September 1993!)

Twelve-year-old Joan was known as 'Little Joan'. Peggy was always called 'Peg', so this saved any confusion when we evacuees, Joan and Peggy, went to live with them. Peg had a bedroom to herself. We four evacuees, together with Little Joan, slept in one large bedroom. The two Joans shared, whilst the other three of us had single beds. However, this was not to last long as Betty and Effie went home after a few weeks.

Daily, after college, Joan and I walked the dog, 'Gyp', in the pine woods and meadow nearby. We often saw one of the school boys from the grammar school out with his dog. He and his friend sometimes accompanied us home that lovely autumn, riding their bicycles. When we returned, after the war, to visit our billet, we learned that while the young man was abroad in the forces in 1944, a

V2 rocket fell directly on his parents' house.   Tragically, both they
and the dog were killed.

Chapter Two

Cold and Deprivation

For our studies we used a hired room over the offices of an estate agent. The room was large and heated only by an old-fashioned coal fireplace. Each morning the fire was lit by a cleaner before we arrived. Our first winter, 1939/40, was bitterly cold, with thick snow lying for weeks. Joan and I used to go home for our main meal at midday, trudging eight miles a day (thirteen kilometres). There were no duffel coats then, just woollen material topcoats and scarves.

On our feet we wore wellington boots or rubber overshoes, and we suffered the most terrible chilblains on our toes and ankles. The only known remedy was to soak our feet in water as hot as we could bear. This did not seem to help much and, in addition, left our feet very tender. We tried an old-fashioned balm called 'Sno-creme', still with little effect.

The pond nearby was frozen over so Mr M borrowed some ice-skates for himself and the three of us. By holding hands we managed to skate over the ice with no mishaps. It was quite exciting and exhilarating, on a lovely moonlit night, to ice-skate for the first time.

Apart from a downstairs bathroom, in which also stood a boiler for clothes-washing, our personal washing facilities were quite primitive. Each morning a large jug of hot water, which we shared between us, was brought up to our bedroom. We washed out of an old-fashioned china bowl. With no heating, the bedroom was bitterly cold in winter, but we survived this somehow.

It was to our great relief when the hard winter was over at long last. Little did we know that this would not compare with our relief at the end of the following winter of the 1940/41 Blitz.

Chapter Three

Spring Comes to the Countryside

In the spring of 1940, Beryl, aged ten, who was in the preparatory department, joined us in our billet. She too trekked the eight miles each day to and from our improvised classroom, usually sustained by sweets she bought en route. (Sweets were later rationed.) On one visit of her parents, her mother asked me to take Beryl to a local shop to buy a 'play' outfit for her. This seemed to me a great responsibility, but fortunately we found some navy shorts and a coloured, striped top (today's 'T-shirt') which fitted perfectly. To my great relief, Beryl's mother was very pleased and said she couldn't have chosen better herself. She credited me with the choice, though I remember having felt grateful to the helpful young shop assistant. This outfit cost less than five shillings (25p)!

Clothing rationing came in soon after that. My two elder sisters said they would borrow some of my coupons and repay them when I commenced work. (Of course, they never did!) Identity cards were issued to everyone. Food rationing started.

Our breaks from college were quite short: ten days at Christmas and Easter, with three weeks in the summer. Our hours were 9.30 a.m. to 4.30 p.m., with a two-hour break for lunch. This gave us time to walk the four miles to and from our billet for our midday meal.

Wednesday afternoons were free for recreation. When the weather was fine, we either all went on a countryside ramble, or played tennis in the grounds of the house where our tutor was staying. Other Wednesdays, we sometimes went swimming.

Before the war, Mr M had been a member of the town band. He also led the local boys' brigade band. Some Sundays, usually when there was a church parade, we attended. Before and after the service we would listen to their rather ear-splitting but well-intentioned renderings on wind instruments and drums. One Sunday morning we decided to walk round Knowle Park. Little Joan, Beryl, Joan and I, together with Gyp the dog, walked the two and a half miles to the park and around its five to six mile stone-walled perimeter. After a while Beryl was tired so I 'piggy-backed' her a few miles. Apart from one corner which held an apparently deserted army encampment, we had the park to ourselves, meeting no one. We eventually reached the gates to the town again, where we found a welcome water fountain. A little further on was an old horse trough where our poor, gasping dog, Gyp, satisfied his thirst at last. At this point I managed to persuade Beryl to jump off my back and walk the remaining couple of miles which, thankfully, were downhill. We had walked over ten miles (sixteen kilometres) that morning, with no watches to tell us the time. Luckily we arrived home, together with a rather bedraggled dog, in time to find the traditional roast Sunday dinner awaiting us. Having had nothing at all to eat since we left some hours before, this meal was more than welcome.

We all felt tired and foot-sore, but satisfied, having achieved our endeavour. Gyp slept for the rest of the day!

Chapter Four

War on the Home Front

Beryl left us after a couple of months. Soon after, in the summer of 1940, came the miraculous evacuation of our troops from Dunkirk in France. Every boat, large and small, was rallied to bring them home across the Channel. This heralded the end of the 'Phoney War'. The Kent coast started to be shelled badly by night and day. Three or four relatives left their homes in Walmer, near Dover, to avoid the heavy shelling and came to live with us for a few weeks. How nine or even ten of us managed in a small three-bedroomed house, I shall always wonder. The tablecloth was never off the large table – no eating out for us in those days!

Some Saturdays, my sister Betty would cycle down for the day when we went out for a picnic. Betty would bring fruit pies (4d each – 1½p), which she had bought at one of the Lyons Corner Houses in central London. These eating places were very popular for the spaciousness and comfort, each containing several restaurants. Although the well-presented portions were sufficient, they were never lavish. The exception to this was the restaurant called The Salad Bowl where a sweet, roll and butter and as much salad as desired could be obtained at the cost of half-a-crown (12½p). (The Government permitted meals to be obtained up to the value of 5 sh. (25p) per person.) At all the other Corner House restaurants waitresses served, being always smartly dressed in dark coloured outfits topped with dainty white caps and aprons. They were known as 'Nippies'. There was also a food hall which sold limited quantities of delicacies, including the pies which Betty and I took on our walks in the lovely Kent countryside. These tasty baked morsels proved a special treat.

Once, when the invasion was expected, we were walking through the woods and found a cordon across the path. We were promptly sent back by military policemen. This added excitement to our day.

Undeterred, by walking unseen through the wooded undergrowth we reached our goal anyway – and not a German in sight!

Sunday was the highlight of our week. My friend Joan's parents eked out their petrol ration to drive down to see us. Also, Sunday was the day we had a cooked breakfast of our week's ration of one egg and one or two rashers of bacon. (Later in the war this was reduced to one egg per fortnight.) Tea, which was shared with our two visitors, included lettuce and beetroot grown in the garden and the special treat of cake.

Sometimes they would bring my parents down to see me. My father was an assistant stage manager in London. Most theatres closed down during the Blitz, so times were not easy. My pocket money was sent fortnightly by way of a 3 sh. (15p) postal order. Joan was luckier, and her kind mother would give me a 6d piece (2½p), which was appreciated beyond words.

Joan's parents, who ran fish shops, used to bring large portions of fish and chips which we ate at midday on Mondays. Being used to wartime rationing, we found that walking the two miles back to college proved quite an effort after such a filling meal!

We went home that summer of 1940, as usual. All was peaceful until the day of my cousin's wedding, to which my family and I were invited.

Just after the reception, which was held in the ballroom of a local department store, we heard the air raid sirens, for the first time since that September day almost a year earlier. The raid was on the East End docks, the first of many to be made on London. We were all advised to go to the basement until the all-clear sounded, which we did, together with the many shoppers, it being a Saturday. We heard nothing, but obviously it 'put a damper' on what we had hoped would be a lovely day for my cousin and her groom. Within a few months they were bombed out of their home.

On arriving back at Sevenoaks again, we decided to join a newly formed youth club. After a few meetings we held a 'Saturday Hop'. After an hour or so the air raid warning sounded and we had to finish early. On the way home, looking across the North Downs, we saw a bright red glow stretching all over the sky. This was the first of the many firebomb raids London was to receive. We just hoped our own homes had not been attacked. (I learned later that several incendiary bombs had fallen around our house. In his anxiety to throw sand over one, my father had lost grip of the box holding the sand, which, being made of wood, created an even bigger bonfire! However, he did not worry unduly, deciding that it would hardly be noticed in that inferno! Several unexploded incendiary bombs were later found on the roof.)

My sister Betty, together with others, regularly took a van round the bombed sites in London and provided tea for the grateful firemen. After little sleep she somehow found the energy to cycle the ten miles or so each morning, up to the City. Overnight bombing of railways, as well as of roads (many of which had tram-lines destroyed), caused havoc with public transport. Cycling was the only way Betty could ensure reaching her office every day of the Blitz.

Whilst my friend Joan and I were at home for the summer holiday, an air raid dugout shelter had been made in the field backing onto the garden of our billet.

During our walks to and from college, we watched the Battle of Britain being fought in the blue skies of summer 1940. From the famous Biggin Hill airfield not far away came our Spitfire and Hurricane fighters weaving in and out, attacking the German bombers. We cheered when they were successful in bringing one down. Sometimes we saw one of our aircraft spinning to earth and tried to pretend to ourselves that it was not one of ours.

My friend Joan's brother, Ken Davis, was trained as a pilot in the Royal Air Force, but a year later his aircraft came down over Norway. His family lived in hope for the rest of the war that he was being safely looked after by the Norwegians and secretly kept hidden from the German occupying forces. Sadly, at the end of hostilities, they were to learn that he and his crew and been killed in the crash. They had been buried by the Norwegians, to be moved to an official grave after the war. He was just twenty years of age.

At college, if our lessons were interrupted by the sirens, we all went outside to a dugout shelter, but were more interested in trying to watch the air battles overhead. When an aircraft was heard coming down, we were ushered into safety, mainly in case the enemy plane was still loaded with its deadly weapons. In between alerts we continued our studies.

In the evenings, before the night raids started, we listened to the radio. The comedians of the day did their utmost to keep up our morale and make us laugh. Our favourite broadcast was at 8 p.m. on Saturdays, called *Band Wagon* with Arthur Askey and Richard ('Dicky') Murdoch. Each Sunday, before the news, the national anthem of all the countries which had fallen under the heel of the Nazis were played. The list seemed endless.

The nation listened to the speeches of the new prime minister, Mr Winston Churchill. He praised 'The Few' (our Battle of Britain fighter pilots), telling us we must expect 'Blood, sweat, toil and tears' in our stand against the enemy and that we would 'never surrender'.

During the day raids there was the threat of invasion of our Isles. Rumour even had it that the Germans had landed. We were told to expect to see their tanks coming along the road where we were billeted, it being the one leading from Maidstone and the coast to London. Thankfully, the Germans decided to drop their plans to invade – named by them, 'Operation Sea Lion'. (Could they have heard of our Home Guard – 'Dad's Army'?!)

Mr M became an air raid warden, being on duty one night a week at his post just along the road. Blackout precautions had been carried out by order of the Government at the beginning of the war. At our billet, these consisted of plywood with wooden surrounds which fitted into, and covered the window. They were very effective, so we never heard the threatening call, 'Put that light out!'

At my home the windows were regularly blown out. Eventually these were replaced by only a small pane of glass set into a wide wooden surround. These made the rooms very dull and depressing to live in for the duration of the war. The replacements could not have been very securely fixed as I remember during the later flying bomb attack, these too were blown down by the blast.

Chapter Five

The Blitz

As the day raids subsided, the night Blitzkrieg began.

Most 'picture houses' (cinemas) closed temporarily during the Blitz. Joan and I visited the cinema only twice. First, with our tutor and the other students to see a French-speaking film. The second occasion was when we saw a musical – *Strike Up The Band* starring, I believe, Mickey Rooney and Judy Garland. We were 'lost' in this film for a few hours. It was like living in another world and it cheered us up immensely. I recall the anti-climax when we stepped out of the cinema to face the stark reality of war again.

The air raid warning sounded nearly every night from September 1940 to the spring of 1941. Each evening, usually before we even heard the sirens, we would wrap up warm and all six of us would troop down to the dugout shelter which had been prepared for us in the field beyond the garden.

It was almost completely underground, its height and width about six and a half feet (two metres) by twenty feet (six metres) long. At the far end was an emergency exit, a hole just large enough to crawl through if the main entrance had become blocked. Inside, close by, the wire mesh base of a double bed (no mattress!) had been placed across the width of the shelter. On this, the two Joans and myself lay. A large feather bolster cushioned our heads and we each wrapped ourselves up in a blanket. It was very uncomfortable, but we somehow managed to sleep until dawn when the all-clear siren sounded.

Before the improvised bed was installed, we sat on wooden forms. Other members of the family used to join us. All through one night I sat and nursed a baby granddaughter, Jean. I was assured that even if I fell asleep I would find that I would not drop her. Nevertheless, I don't think I slept much that night!

We used to listen to the sound of the engines of the German bombers chugging overhead, almost as though their loads of bombs were too heavy for their aircraft. They certainly seemed to pass overhead much faster on the return journey from bombing London! Anti-aircraft guns and barrage balloons helped defend our cities.

After midnight they would come back for another attack. It now appears that the same air crews were used for both missions. They would return to the continent to refuel and reload with bombs. So we were more accurate than we realised when, in the early hours, we used to say, 'Here they are, coming back again.'

There were rumours of a mad old lady (some even called her a witch!), who started bonfires at night to guide the Nazi bombers. These were lit on a large allotment about a quarter of a mile from us. We could not understand why the 'witch' was not easily caught. The reason was kept very secret. As we learned after the war, bonfires were lit as decoys, deliberately to mislead the Germans. Presumably so they would think they were their own flares which had been dropped to light their targets. This would cause them to distribute their bombs outside London instead of on it. Whether this ruse worked, I doubt. As far as I know there were only two incidents locally. One was a direct hit on a large hall in the centre of Sevenoaks town. Only the night before, so we heard, the hall had been full of sleeping soldiers!

The only other local incident I was aware of occurred one night when, because I was not feeling too well, I was allowed to go upstairs for a rest after tea. When, a few hours later, the sirens went off as usual, I was found fast asleep in bed, so was allowed to stay. This was the night the local high school was bombed not far away. Down in the shelter they thought I would soon be joining them. All I did was get under the bedclothes to smother the noise, then I had the best night's sleep for weeks, in a lovely, comfortable bed for a change. I felt really refreshed the next morning, but was not allowed to do that again!

We all went home for the Christmas holidays as usual. One day, when my sister Betty and I went to visit our eldest sister Marjorie, we could not get home because the Blitz had started early. A railway junction not far away was one of the Luftwaffe's targets that night. We all settled down in the 'safest' room away from windows. Marjorie and her husband, George, were on the fireside rug; sister Betty and I lay with our heads on a settee, with four chairs to support us. The house shook occasionally from nearby bombs and the anti-aircraft fire from our guns seemed deafening. Fortunately, we did not have any windows blown out, as we had rather expected. Nevertheless, it was a somewhat uncomfortable and disturbing night.

On Christmas Day my aunt, uncle and cousin Bill came and stayed the night. During the evening my cousin and I walked the dog. Thankfully, the Germans gave us a respite that night, and the silence and peacefulness of the starlit sky seemed almost uncanny. Unfortunately, this one Christmas night of serenity was not to last. On Boxing Day the raids resumed with renewed fury.

The bombing was particularly severe on the last day of my Christmas holidays. I had little sleep, but duly caught the Green Line coach back to Sevenoaks the next morning. Arriving late back at college, I was welcomed with relief. All through the Blitz, Joan and I never missed a day of college.

Chapter Six

Respite and Rationing

The spring of 1941 came at last and we then had a respite from air raids for over a year. We were able to concentrate more on our studies and take our RSA (Royal Society of Arts) examinations. Bus passes were obtained for us to ride two of our journeys to or from college each day, leaving us just over four miles to walk.

At our billet, most of our meals were cooked in an oven beside a coal fire which also served to heat the living room as well. Economy was the order of the day throughout the war. This included fuel, which was required for the war industry.

At my home there was often only a very low grade of coal available. This was officially called 'nutty slack' and consisted of a mixture of nut-size pieces of coal and coal dust which created more smoke than heat. Coal fires were almost invariably the only form of domestic heating and the intermittent shortage of coal caused great discomfort in many homes.

Food had been rationed since mid-1940.

Our weekly rations generally consisted of eight ounces (225 grammes) each of sugar and jam, four ounces each of bacon and butter (or margarine), two ounces each of tea, cheese and cooking fat. Meat to the value of 1 sh. 1d plus one egg. Two pints of milk were allowed as a minimum – extra being allowed if available. Any commodity off the ration, such as fish, sausages and certain groceries, could only be obtained by queuing. Some scant foods could also, if you were lucky, be obtained 'under the counter', as it was known, where these precious commodities were hidden from view. Few people had time to queue, except for the resolute mothers who did all they could to cater for their families. Many of them followed the advice which was broadcast over the radio by the Ministry of Food experts. This included possible menus to help eke out the rations.

In large towns, on the corner of each road, was placed a receptacle called a 'pig bin'. In this my mother, along with many others, placed any unwanted scraps such as rinds or stale bread. These were collected daily by the local council, to be used as valuable food for pigs, thus ensuring our meagre bacon ration.

The German U-boats (submarines) were, for a long while, winning the battle against our merchant navy. At one time, apparently, Britain stood alone, with only two weeks' supply of food. Every vegetable grown at home, or scrap saved, was vital to our survival.

My mother regularly met her two sisters shopping. One afternoon they were idly standing outside a shop having a chat before going home their separate ways. (The shop was closed, as often happened when traders had sold out and were awaiting further supplies.) Deep in conversation, they suddenly looked round and found that a queue had formed behind them. With some amusement they had to explain that they were just talking together, and not standing waiting for the shop to open! With obvious disappointment, but in good humour, the queue dispersed.

Our diet became very monotonous. At our billet there was always bread, which was unrationed. (It was in the immediate post-war years of austerity that its rationing commenced. After the financial strain of the war, the country was bankrupt.) With an ample supply of vegetables being grown in the garden and allotment, we never felt hungry. This self-sufficiency supported the Government's 'Dig for Victory' campaign – the victory we never doubted! Meat was rationed to 1 sh. 1d (5½p) per person a week. The butcher delivered to our billet every Saturday, when we were favoured to have sausages for dinner. (Some people were encouraged to eat whale-meat!)

In the autumn, on our walks down the lanes, we collected apples and Kent cob nuts, which we ate with relish.

Saturday mornings, we helped in the house. Joan cleaned the silver cutlery and I tidied the living room. In the afternoon we usually walked the one and a half miles up into the town and shops. Our main interest was Woolworth's, it being within our price range. We often just browsed but sometimes made purchases such as embroidery silks (1d per skein!). Small tray-cloths to embroider could still be bought for about one shilling. White cotton ankle socks cost 6d (2½p) per pair.

We were delighted when we were given a large quantity of khaki coloured wool from the local WRVS (Women's Royal Voluntary Service). All our spare time was spent knitting gloves, mittens, socks and balaclava helmets for the forces.

In the summer of 1941 Peg joined the ATS (Auxiliary Territorial Service) to serve on an 'ack-ack' (anti-aircraft) site 'somewhere in Britain'. Everyone strictly kept the movement of troops at home and abroad very 'hush-hush', so locations were never mentioned. Wherever one went there were to be seen posters reading 'Careless talk costs lives', which was quite a daunting thought. We missed Peg when she was 'called up', as, despite everything, we had managed quite a few laughs.

As the days became shorter, some neighbours came in each evening for a game of darts, which made a happy contrast to our life during the previous winter of the Blitzkrieg.

Chapter Seven

Home for Good!

We went home to a very austere Christmas. No turkeys were available but we felt lucky to get a piece of pork to roast, to be followed by the plainest of Christmas puddings. Also, we were given the sad news that Joan's brother had not returned from a flying mission over Norway.

It was at this Christmas homecoming that my parents told me that, as my course would be finishing later in 1942, I would be leaving Sevenoaks and returning to my local home college for the final months. It was with some sadness that I returned to Sevenoaks with the news. However, this was soon overridden by the excitement of going home again for good.

The war, though, was less than half over. We had yet to face the 'Little Blitz' of the winter of 1942/43, when I was working in the City of London in marine insurance. The V1 flying bombs (called 'doodlebugs'), followed by the V2 rockets, came in 1944 and early 1945, when I had been 'called up' to the Air Ministry in central London.

In May 1945, soon after the end of my teenage years, the peace treaty was signed in Germany and all hostilities in Europe ceased. At last, on the national holiday of VE Day, we were able to celebrate the long-awaited and yearned-for victory in Europe.